T0266226

Be Your
Best Self

*Joysa Maben Winter
and Mark H. Levine*

BEHRMAN HOUSE

Behrman House, Inc.
www.behrmanhouse.com

In gratitude to the teachers who have inspired my journey:
  Rabbi Marc Boone Fitzerman
  Rabbi Stephen Fuchs
  Rabbi Stephen Booth-Nadav

                    Joysa Maben Winter

With gratitude to the Holy One of blessing, who blessed
  me with Joshua, Jesse, and Dahlia

                    Mark H. Levine

Project Manager: **Barbara D. Krasner**
Design: **Jill A. Winitzer**

The publisher gratefully acknowledges the following sources of photographs:
Nir Darom, page ii; leonello calvetti, Monkey Business Images, page iii; BIELOUS NATALIIA , page 3; maxim-mmmum, Eugene Ivanov, page 4; Joan Roth (1994), page 6; Library of Congress, National Photo Company Collection, page7; Istomina Olena, page 8; Luba, page 9; Lena Sergeeva, Oksvik, pages 11, 21, 31, 41; dslaven, Mikhail Levit /Shutterstock.com, page 12; joyart, page 16; Beit T'Shuvah, page 17; Bridgeman Art Library, page 18; Eugene Ivanov, page 19; Natalia Sheinkin, page 20; Gabriela Insuratelu, pages 22, 23; thumb, Yiannis Papadimitriou, page 24; Donna Beeler, page 28; EyeTech Digital Systems, page 27; red-feniks, page 32-33; The Archives of the YIVO Institute for Jewish Research, New York, page 36; Library of Congress, Agnes Elizabeth Ernst Meyer papers, 37; Maugli, page 38; Elena Elisseeva, page 39; Ralph Biggör, page 40; Monkey Business Images, pages 42-43.

CONTENTS

INTRODUCTION

Eating a challah, hearing a shofar, and sitting at the Seder table are probably three of your earliest Jewish memories. Psychologists tell us that you remember these things because each one is associated with a strong, physical sensation: the sweet taste of the challah, the piercing sound of the shofar, and the colorful sight of foods on the Pesach table.

On a more profound level, however, these rituals are meaningful because they connect us to Jewish history. Eating challah on Shabbat reminds us of the manna God provided our ancestors as they wandered helplessly in the wilderness. Listening to the shofar on Rosh Hashanah recalls the primitive, agricultural lifestyle of the ancient Jewish community. And reclining at the Seder table prompts us to imagine that we participated in the exodus from Egypt.

But the most significant aspect of Jewish rituals is that these practices symbolize values we hold sacred. For example, reciting the blessing for the challah on Shabbat and holidays draws our attention to the belief that God is the ultimate Creator of the world. The shrill cry of the shofar awakens us to the principle that regular self-examination leads to a fuller and richer life, and reciting the haggadah each Pesach celebrates the values of physical and spiritual freedom.

At times, however, Jewish values conflict with contemporary American values. For instance, American society glorifies individualism and personal success. Americans measure success by the size of their bank accounts and the brand names on their acquisitions. These advertising messages bombard us every day in books, commercials, billboards, and Hollywood blockbusters.

Traditional Jewish values, on the other hand, are different. Judaism praises humility—thinking modestly about our own importance and position in society. Judaism reminds us that the talents or gifts we possess do not come from us. They come from powers or forces outside us, such as God, our family, or the simple windfall of good luck.

The Living Jewish Values series introduces some of the most important—and sus-

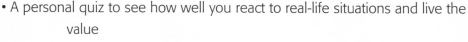

taining—values of our tradition. In this first volume, Be Your Best Self, we examine four values that underlie personal enrichment and growth:

K'vod Habriyot—Individual Dignity

T'shuvah—Returning to Your Best Self

Sameach B'Chelko—Personal Satisfaction

Anavah—Humility

Each chapter includes:

• A personal quiz to see how well you react to real-life situations and live the value

• A Talmudic or present-day story that demonstrates the "Agaddic Tradition"

• A profile of a "Superstar" man or woman who has embodied the particular value

• A glimpse into the past to learn how the value has stood the test of time

• Activities to help you apply what you've learned

• An opportunity for you to journal your thoughts and reflections

Throughout this book, you'll have the opportunity to think about what these values mean to you, whether they have influenced your beliefs, and in what new ways you might bring them into your life.

Challahs are eaten. Shofars split and crack. But the morals at the heart of our tradition live on forever—as long as we continue to teach and continue to learn.

CHAPTER 1

K'vod Habriyot

Rabbi Jeremiah heard that Rabbi Abba had a complaint against him, so he went to his home to apologize. While R. Jeremiah waited outside his colleague's door, a maidservant tossed filthy waste water from a window into the dung heap on the ground. Some of it splashed on Jeremiah's head. The instant Rabbi Abba heard what had happened, he rushed outside. Rabbi Jeremiah began to apologize, but Rabbi Abba interrupted him, pleading: "No, do not beg forgiveness! Now it is my job to make you forget this humiliation."

The Babylonian Talmud, Tractate Yoma

Individual Dignity

When the ancient sages who wrote the Talmud looked for an example of כְּבוֹד הַבְּרִיּוֹת (*k'vod habriyot*), the importance of individual dignity, they chose the story of Rabbi Jeremiah's humiliation. Although we no longer relate to the details that make this tale compelling—thankfully, our houses have plumbing—its message still speaks to us: The dignity of all humans must be preserved and treasured.

A modern example of public humiliation would definitely feature smart-phones, text messages, and the Internet, because these technologies provide instantaneous (and sometimes anonymous) opportunities to hurt people's feelings or damage their reputations.

Consider Hannah, a fifth-grader who snapped a picture on her phone of her classmate Bonnie's shoes, which she thought were ugly. Hannah forwarded the picture to her friend Haley, and Haley forwarded it to five other people. Before the end of the day, the whole school was laughing at the picture and teasing Bonnie whenever they saw her.

EVERYONE WANTS TO BELONG

UNFORTUNATELY, stories like this happen regularly. Rosalind Wiseman, who wrote *Queen Bees and Wannabes*, a book that explores cruelty inside social cliques, explains that bullying happens because kids want to feel like they belong.

"The easiest way to feel a part of a group is to see people outside your group as different." says Wiseman. "Your group starts feeling superior to others, and soon you believe that people outside your group don't deserve respect." Jewish tradition combats this type of petty meanness. Rabbi Eliezer teaches in Pirkei Avot, "Let the dignity of others be as dear to you as your own."

ACTIVITY 1

STAMP OUT BULLYING

 RT @rabbiEliezer **"Let your friend's honor be as dear to you as your own."** #PirkeiAvot

Identify three causes of bullying _____
_____
_____

Identify two effects of bullying _____
_____

Identify three solutions to the problem _____
_____

Why are these good solutions? _____
_____

How does Rabbi Eliezer's advice help solve the problem of bullying?
_____
_____
_____
_____

Do You Treat People with Dignity?

Take this quiz. Record how many blue, green, or red responses you have, and find out.

Your elderly great-aunt loves to tell you stories, but she often repeats the same story. When she visits, you:

◆ Excuse yourself and go out with a friend.

◆ Spend time with her and act interested in what she says.

◆ Stay for a while, and then find something else to do.

When you're with your friends and see the school janitor, what do you do?

◆ Say hello and continue talking to your friends.

◆ Pass by without saying hello because your friends take all your attention.

◆ Stop to ask how he is and encourage your friends to do the same.

In the school cafeteria, the server doesn't speak much English. When she serves lunch, you:

◆ Order food patiently and try to make conversation in simple English.

◆ Ask for your food politely and move on.

◆ Expect her to understand you, and get annoyed when you have to repeat yourself.

A.J. has some learning problems. At recess one day, she asks for help with an assignment you think is really easy. What do you say?

◆ "Sorry, this is my free time. I want to relax."

◆ "Show me what the problem is, and I will be happy to help."

◆ "I don't think I can help you since I'm not that good at explaining things."

Mostly blue
Lovey Lucy
"Love people and honor them!" (*Derech Eretz Zuta 1*). You appreciate other people and try hard to show it. This is a great character trait to keep cultivating!

Mostly green
Middle of the Road Marlo
It is sometimes hard for you to treat others with dignity. Perhaps you are shy or worry about what people think of you. When you find yourself about to say or do something harsh, challenge yourself and think, "How else can I respond to this?"

Mostly red
Nervous Nellie
You can have a critical eye and lose patience with people who don't meet your standards. The more experience you have meeting people who are different from you, the more comfortable you will be. And remember, doing or saying something that makes you *uncomfortable* can be okay—it might mean you are learning something new!

AGADDIC TRADITION

It was only after a terrible tragedy that I became aware of the Carlebach Shul in Manhattan. My 18-year-old son was killed in a car accident. I was devastated. I came from a secular Jewish background and never cared about religion. But suddenly, for the first time in my life, I needed spiritual help.

Rabbi Shlomo Carlebach of the Carlebach Shul in Manhattan took me under his wing. I began going to all of his gatherings. One night, I showed up at the synagogue, not knowing he had a concert scheduled. I didn't have a penny in my pocket.

I thought about sneaking in, but someone was guarding the door like a lion, collecting the $10 fee. I considered begging him to let me in, but he looked like the kind of person who would never give a "freebie."

Just then, I saw Rabbi Carlebach. Telling him my situation, I asked, "Can you sneak me in?" He looked at me thoughtfully and said, "Why don't you come upstairs?"

His home was a simple suite of rooms above the synagogue. I thought he was leading me to a secret door, where he could sneak me in, but instead he started hunting around. After tossing many things aside, he found what he wanted: a pouch with many zippered sections.

After opening each one and finding it empty, he opened the last section and pulled out a $10 bill. "There!" he said, with a big smile. "Now you can buy a ticket!" I went back downstairs and gave the man the $10. I entered the hall, my dignity intact.

— Adapted from the book Holy Brother: *Inspiring Stories and Enchanted Tales about Rabbi Shlomo Carlebach*

ACTIVITY 2

It could have been easier for Rabbi Carlebach to give the man permission to enter the concert free of charge.
Why did he give him money? _____
_____
_____

Why does the writer say his dignity was "still intact?" _____
_____
_____

This story is about "losing face."
Have you been in a situation where you "lost face?" Have you seen it happen to someone else? What actions would have preserved dignity in that situation? _____
_____
_____
_____

K'VOD HABRIYOT SUPERSTAR

On **March 25, 1911,** at 4:45 p.m., someone on the eighth floor of the Triangle Shirtwaist Factory in New York City carelessly dropped a match on a pile of fabric. Instantly, flames engulfed the workers, who ran frantically to the stairway, the elevator, and the fire escape. As the deadly curtain of fire spread to the ninth floor, employees fled to the exits, only to find the doors locked. Their only hope for survival rested on the shoulders of fire fighters, who quickly arrived on the scene. Tragically, the ladders on the fire trucks could not reach above the sixth floor, and the water from the hoses fell far short of the upper floors.

Thousands of horror-stricken people watched from below as dozens of young women leaped to their deaths rather than burn alive. By day's end, 146 people had died. The disaster angered the country, but the Jewish community was particularly distraught. Most of the dead were young, immigrant Jewish women. Not surprisingly, labor reform emerged as a hotbed of Jewish communal activism.

STANDING UP FOR DIGNITY

At the center of that activism stood Rose Schneiderman, a young Jewish woman who dedicated her life to fighting for workers' dignity. Born in Poland, Rose immigrated to America in 1890 at the age of eight. When she was in sixth grade, her father died, and she dropped out of school to support her family. Rose learned firsthand that garment workers in sweatshops were stripped of their dignity. They endured long hours and cramped working conditions. Her early experiences fueled her passion for labor reform and motivated her to organize women in labor unions.

During a memorial event for the victims of the Triangle Shirtwaist Factory fire, Rose delivered a spellbinding speech, urging women workers to unionize.

"This is not the first time girls have been burned alive in the city. Every week I must learn of the untimely death of one of my sister workers. The life of men and women is so cheap, and property is so sacred. There are so many of us for one job, it matters little if 146 of us are burned to death ... I know from my experience it is up to the working people to save themselves. The only way they can save themselves is by a strong working-class movement."

Over many generations, Jews developed the practice of writing to religious authorities with ethical and legal questions about how to live according to Jewish law. This style of question and response is known as *She'elot U'Teshuvot* (Questions and Answers), and it continues today. Below are two questions that might have been posed about real problems that certain communities faced in history.

Before you read the answers, see if you can resolve the dilemmas in ways that best preserve individual dignity.

Question #1: Land of the Lovelorn

May our Teacher instruct us in this:

I live in a small, thriving community in Russia, but like most of my neighbors, I'm very poor. My daughter is approaching marriageable age, and I'm worried she won't be able to attract a suitable match. Although she is a delightful person, her clothes are shabby and worn.

Marriage!

Our community observes an ancient custom that was celebrated by our ancestors, of blessed memory, on the 15th of Av. On this day each year, the daughters of Jerusalem would go and dance in the vineyards under the full moon. The men would also go, and whoever did not have a wife would go there to find a bride. So it is in our village.

Unfortunately, the available bachelors in our village are attracted to wealthy girls whose families can afford stylish dresses. As a result, my daughter, and the daughters of many poor families, remain single.

What should we do?

Habriyot in History

Question #2: "Come On Up — and Good Luck!"

May our Teacher instruct us in this:

It is 5,361 years since the creation of the world. We are a large Jewish community living in the great bounty of the Rhineland (Germany).

But despite our large numbers and the many blessings bestowed upon us by God, we struggle to fulfill the mitzvah of reading the Torah aloud before the congregation because so few people can read Hebrew, our holy language.

How can we continue to fulfill this sacred mitzvah?

Response to Question #1:
Land of the Lovelorn

If the matter is as your letter of inquiry states, it seems to us as follows:

Because it is embarrassing for a young woman wearing ragged clothes to dance and compete beside a woman in fancy clothes during the 15th of Av celebration, we have decided as follows:

On the morning of the 15th of Av, all women in the community shall exchange their clothing. Thus, when they dance under the full moon, no one will be able to distinguish between the rich and the poor.

Response to Question #2:
"Come On Up — and Good Luck!"

If the matter is as your letter of inquiry states, it seems to us as follows:

We learn in the Talmud that when pilgrims came to the Temple with their First Fruit Offerings, they were required to read a few verses. Because not everyone could read, the practice was changed, and a permanent reader was assigned to read for everyone. Therefore, people would not be embarrassed because they could not read. Everyone's dignity was maintained. We suggest you adopt the practice. Assign a permanent Torah reader and give others the honor of reciting the blessings.

ACTIVITY 3

On the lines of the Fishbone diagram,
write behaviors that will fulfill **Ben Zoma**'s famous saying.

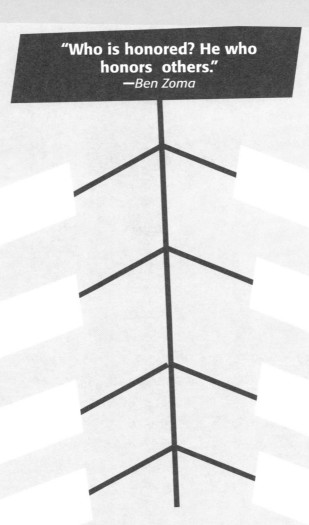

"Who is honored? He who
honors others."
—*Ben Zoma*

*Each person
possesses infinite value and is
entitled to infinite respect and concern.*

WHAT I THINK

Jewish tradition teaches that all humans are created *b'tzelem Elohim* (in the image of God). Therefore, when we treat others with less dignity than they deserve, we diminish the presence of God in the world. This guiding principle has shaped Jewish life for centuries.

1. Describe a time when you were bullied. How did you react? How would you react now?

2. How has your experience with bullying affected who you are?

3. Describe what the world would be like if everyone recognized that we're made in the image of God.

4. Have you ever intentionally embarrassed someone in public? What were the circumstances?

5. If you could say something to that person today, what would you say?

CHAPTER 2

T'shuvah RETURNING

A midrash teaches:

"**A king's child** was sick, and the doctor said that if the child would eat a certain thing, healing would be certain. But the child was too frightened to eat it. The king said to the child, 'So you may know that it will not harm you, I will eat of it.' [Similarly] God said to Israel, 'You are ashamed [and frightened] to repent; behold, I will be the first to repent,' as it is written (Jeremiah 30:18): 'Thus says Adonai, Behold I will turn.'"

TO YOUR BEST SELF

Our sages understood that תְּשׁוּבָה (*t'shuvah*, returning to your highest self) might cause pain; after all, it requires an honest examination of our behavior and a sincere acceptance of our misdeeds. Therefore, to inspire the community to begin the difficult practice of *t'shuvah*, the midrash introduces a radical idea: God not only desires *t'shuvah* from us, but the Creator performs *t'shuvah* first.

Today, the notion of God analyzing Divine behavior and admitting mistakes seems incredible. So, we must look for deeper meanings in the tale. One interpretation explains that when the sages wanted to teach the importance of a specific behavior, they attributed it to God. By doing so, they elevated the behavior to a special status. If so, then the lesson we should learn from our midrash is that *t'shuvah* is valuable and worthy of undertaking.

OVERCOMING THE OBSTACLES TO *T'SHUVAH*

The word *t'shuvah* is often translated as repentance, but it really means "turning" or "returning." When we put *t'shuvah* into practice, we turn *away* from mistakes *toward* more honorable actions. In other words, we return to our better self, the person we were meant to be.

But beware. *T'shuvah* is difficult. Each of us has the capacity for self-improvement, renewal, and growth. And each of us has the capacity for anger, dishonesty and selfishness. That which tempts us to embrace our lesser qualities is called the yetzer hara, the evil impulse. That which helps us embrace our better selves is called *yetzer ha tov*—the good impulse.

Our task each day is to embrace the yetzer ha tov and to resist the *yetzer hara*. To realize our best self.

 RT @BenZoma: "Who is strong? Those who overpower their evil inclinations." #Pirkei Avot

ACTIVITY 1

Through careful planning, you can steer clear of temptation when it blocks your path to t'shuvah. Use the chart below to jot down some strategies you can use to stay true to your best self.

Example:
I won't condemn myself for being imperfect. All humans make mistakes.

Strategies I will use to resist the *yetzer hara* and become my best self

Example:
I will take little steps toward improvement and not get frustrated.

Are You on the Path to *T'shuvah?*

Take this quiz. Record how many blue, green or red responses you have, and find out.

You are sitting with friends at lunch when Alex passes by. You say nothing and Alex sits alone at another table. The next day you:

◆ Apologize to Alex and ask your friends to invite him to join you.

◆ Pretend you don't see Alex passing by.

◆ Invite Alex to sit with you, even though you don't have a lot to talk about.

Your brother asks you to play his favorite game, but you want to watch TV and you tell him to go away. He gets upset. You:

◆ Realize he looks up to you, and turn off the TV.

◆ Apologize, but explain that you need to relax.

◆ Watch TV anyway, but help him find something to do by himself first.

You promised to take out the trash but forget and your parents get annoyed. You:

◆ Collect the trash immediately, but complain about it the whole time.

◆ Say "sorry," and go collect the trash.

◆ Promise to do it first thing in the morning. You write a note to remind yourself.

The day before a science project is due, you still haven't done your part. Your project partner, Adiel, gets angry and ends up doing your work. You:

◆ Apologize to Adiel, but explain that it wasn't your fault—you were so busy this week! You promise to do better next time.

◆ Say "sorry" and explain that you got so wrapped up in your own life, you just forgot about it. "I won't let it happen again," you say.

◆ Get angry at her. Adiel shouldn't be judging you—she has no idea how much else you had going on this week.

Mostly blue
The Introspector
You are an introspective person who carefully considers your own actions. You understand the first step of *t'shuvah*—disliking your own actions. You also sometimes admit that you have done wrong,, *vidui* (confession). You are well on your way to embracing *t'shuvah*.

Mostly green
The Deep Thinker
You try to correct your mistakes. At times, you struggle to understand other peoples' point of view, and you feel uncertain about what upsets them. You are headed down the right *t'shuvah* path.

Mostly red
Master of Maneuvers
You are masterful at satisfying other peoples' needs while getting a portion of what you want. This healthy skill saves you from always sacrificing your needs for others. Your challenge, however, is to give more generously of yourself.

AGADDIC TRADITION

Rabbi Huna said in the name of Rabbi Yose: For 120 years, the Holy One kept warning the generation of the flood in the hope they would repent. When they did not repent, God said to Noah, "Make an ark of cedarwood."

Noah planted cedars. When people asked him why he was planting cedars, Noah said, "Because the Holy One is going to bring a flood to destroy the world. God told me to build an ark to escape."

They laughed and made fun of him. Years went by, and Noah kept watering his cedars, which grew from tiny saplings into towering trees. When they asked him again, "What are you doing?" he gave them the same answer. They continued to ridicule him.

Finally, the day came when it was time to cut the cedars down. He cut them into planks and began to build his ark, and people again asked, "What are you doing?"

"I'm doing what I said I would do," Noah said, and again warned them about the flood.

When they did not repent, even then, the Holy One brought the great flood.

At last, when they saw they were about to drown, they tried to overrun the ark. What did the Holy One do then? God surrounded the ark with lions.

ACTIVITY 2

1. If people change their behavior simply because something tragic might happen, is their *t'shuvah* less valid?

2. The sage Maimonides wrote that the person who does *t'shuvah* "is beloved by the Creator … as if he or she had never erred." Contrast his view with the view of this aggadic tale. With whom do you agree?

3. Jewish tradition says that when you wrong another person, you should ask for forgiveness. If refused, you should return two more times seeking forgiveness. If the person you have wronged still refuses, then God will forgive you. Would the author of this story agree?

T'SHUVAH SUPERSTAR

Mark Borovitz grew up angry and bitter. He watched helplessly as his father, who died when Borovitz was 14 years old, struggled to provide for the family. "I thought the world owed me something because it had taken my father," Borovitz says. For 20 years, he lived a life of gambling, insurance fraud, and extortion. "In a word," he says, "I was a thief."

Fortunately, while serving a prison sentence in California, Borovitz met a rabbi who taught him that life's emotional pain is common to everyone. Each person, however, reacts differently and each person has a choice to either live with suffering or end it.

Borovitz chose to end his suffering, and he began the work of *t'shuvah*—returning to his best self. He admitted his errors and worked hard to repair the damage his bad behavior had caused. He developed a plan to avoid or act differently in situations that had previously tempted him to err.

After the tough work of inner examination, Borovitz had turned his life around. Motivated to share his success, he became a rabbi and established Beit T'shuvah, a residential recovery program based on a unique mixture of Torah, traditional Jewish teaching, and modern principles of the 12-Step program of Alcoholics Anonymous in Los Angeles for men coping with addiction.

Rabbi Borovitz finds personal meaning in the Passover story. In Hebrew, the word for Egypt is *mitzrayim*, which means "narrow place." When the Israelites fled Pharaoh and slavery, they escaped from a constricted place to a new place of openness and freedom. Similarly, when we yield to the *yetzer hara*, we become enslaved to our negative behaviors. *T'shuvah*, Rabbi Borovitz says, allows us to escape our personal *mitzrayim*. "The journey is the journey of true introspection, living from the inside out rather than the outside in. The measure of success in life is how good and decent we are, not how much we acquire."

Time Capsule

Judaism understands that humans have a strong tendency toward goodness and an equally powerful inclination toward evil. Reconciling both aspects of our nature has challenged Jewish thinkers throughout history.
Here are two examples of that effort in the form of fictional *She'elot U'Teshuvot*.

Question #1: Evil Appetites Run Wild

May our Teacher instruct us in this:

Life in Spain is difficult. Our community is constantly under attack from those that dislike us. Economic restrictions and heavy taxes are unbearable. I fear that soon we will be expelled from the country. In this ugly environment, I find it difficult to control my yetzer hara, *my evil impulses. I always feel angry, particularly at my children. Although I'm usually not jealous, I resent my friends who have more than I do. I'm squeezed financially and have thought about cheating customers. How can I control my evil tendencies?*

T'shuvah in History

Question #2: Darkness vs. Light

May our Teacher instruct us in this:

Even amidst the beauty of the hills of Safed, I'm plagued by the sitra achra, *which is the dark side of human nature and a place without goodness. From this darkness springs many of my most offensive qualities, such as selfishness and laziness. I've tried to defeat these demons but always have failed. What can I do to win the battle and live in light?*

Response to Question #1: Evil Appetites Run Wild

If the matter is as your letter of inquiry states, it seems to us as follows:

You must understand that the yetzer hara *is natural. We cannot completely eliminate it. Indeed, as our teacher Rabbi Nahman said in Rabbi Samuel's name, "But for the* yetzer hara, *no person would build a house, take a spouse and beget children." (Bereisheet Rabba 9:7) In other words, convert your anger into action that will help the community, and turn your jealousy into behaviors that will benefit your family.*

Remember, our task in life is to balance the power of the yetzer hara with our drive to do good.

Response to Question #2: Darkness vs. Light

If the matter is as your letter of inquiry states, it seems to us as follows:

Your assessment of the sitra achra *is correct: It dwells in darkness and stands opposed to holiness and light. And yet, as our masters of Kabbalah have taught, the* sitra achra *has value for us. It exists to give human beings free choice. In any situation we can choose to follow the moral path—such as honesty and generosity—or we can surrender to our animal instincts—such as selfishness and self-gain. Remember that the Torah counsels, "I have put before you life and death, blessing and curse. Choose life."*

ACTIVITY 3

Beneath the line in each silhouette below, list a negative quality that the yetzer ha'ra tempts you to display. Above the line, write at least two strategies you can adopt to transform the negative behavior into a positive behavior. Here's an example.

Keep a journal to record when I'm impatient, practice deep breathing when I feel impatient.

Impatience

To help you put your strategies in action, use the chart below. List each activity, when you plan to start it, end it, and how long it should last.

ACTIVITIES	START DATE	END DATE	DURATION
Practice deep breathing	October 1	January 1	3 months

WHAT I THINK

T'shuvah is returning to one's better self and fulfilling the mission that God intended for each of us. We have the power to choose the right path, but this choice can often be difficult.

1. Make a list of friends and family with whom you want to feel more closely connected. Next to each name, describe at least one behavior that will improve your relationship with that person.

2. Each night for one week, examine your behavior during the day and describe how it helped you become your best self.

3. Describe your feelings about your relationship with God. How can you make that connection stronger?

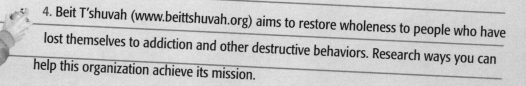

4. Beit T'shuvah (www.beittshuvah.org) aims to restore wholeness to people who have lost themselves to addiction and other destructive behaviors. Research ways you can help this organization achieve its mission.

CHAPTER 3

Sameach B'Chelko

After hearing Alexander the Great boast about his great wealth, our Sages challenged him to pile his gold and silver on one side of a scale and an eyeball on the other. When the heavy treasure could not tip the scale, he added jewels to its weight. Still, the scale would not budge.

"How can this be?" he asked.

The Sages responded, "Your possessions are weighed against the eye of a human being, which is never satisfied."

At the rabbis' suggestion, Alexander covered the eye with dust and only then did the silver and gold tip the scale. (Tamid 32b)

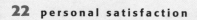

Personal Satisfaction

A gruesome tale? Yes. But the rabbis believed its message was crucial: Our desire for material goods is insatiable. Regardless of what we own, when we see someone with something newer or better, jealousy stirs inside us. Soon, we feel dissatisfied with the belongings that once made us happy.

This insight into human nature led those who crafted our tradition to recognize that happiness will elude us until we learn to say "enough" and embrace the attitude of שָׂמֵחַ בְּחֶלְקוֹ (*sameach b'chelko*, feeling content with who we are and what we have). Adopting this value, however, presents a challenge.

Companies spend billions of dollars every year to market their goods. In fact, some experts estimate that Americans are exposed to at least 3,000 media messages every day. Advertisements try to persuade us that our identity, well-being, and self-esteem depend on buying specific products. In the face of such powerful advertising, cultivating contentment for who we are, and what we have, requires greater effort than merely covering our eyes. Jewish wisdom can help.

Young children often say that they need something when they mean that they want it. But as we mature, we recognize the difference between "needs" and "wants." All humans need food, shelter, and clothing. We might want more or less of these essential needs, but we only require "enough"—that is, neither too little, nor too much.

Distinguishing between wants and needs is the first step toward finding contentment with what we have.

ACTIVITY 1

Draw a line from the objects to the appropriate box.

 RT @Ibn Gabirol Those who seek more than they need hinder themselves from enjoying what they have. #sameach b'chelko

fast food

video gaming system

child care

clothes

fancy car

nutritious food

small car

tennis racket

simple cell phone

apartment

brand name clothes

fancy cell phone

iPod

house

luxury home

skateboard

suitcase

health care

repair costs

computer

concert tickets

NEEDS
the essentials in life that we can't live without

WANTS
items or services that enhance the quality of our lives. Wants can be wasteful if we can't afford them.

What Turns Your Frown Upside Down?

Take this quiz to find out!

In your bedroom, your most prized possession is:

◆ A photo album full of great pics of your friends and counselors from camp.

◆ The trophy from last year's championship basketball game, when you finally hit that hook shot.

◆ Your iPod, which you just couldn't live without.

When you're in a really bad mood, the best way to boost your spirits is to:

◆ Sit down to practice playing your guitar.

◆ Call your best friend, who always knows exactly how to make you laugh.

◆ Get rid of your anger by playing PlayStation.

You just aced a really hard test and are totally psyched. You celebrate by:

◆ Buying that new DVD you've been eyeing.

◆ Going out for ice cream with your parents, who will tell you what a super genius you are.

◆ Blasting your favorite tune and dancing around your room, no matter how silly you look.

A rainy day finally gives you a chance to:

◆ Chill out in front of the TV all afternoon.

◆ Work on your scrapbook, writing little notes and doodling around your favorite memories.

◆ Catch up on e-mail and call your friend who moved out of town.

Mostly blue
Toys and Trinkets
You stay on top of the hottest trends and take pleasure in owning things that everyone is talking about. Even so, you wonder if complete happiness can ever be found in material objects.

Mostly red
Crafts and Creativity
You thrive on physical activity and artistic expression. You wish, as it says in Psalm 90, that inspiration will flow through you, and the work of your hands will prosper.

Mostly green
Friends and Family
Spending time with other people makes you happy, and you cherish these special relationships. You've taken the words of Hillel to heart, putting your energy toward loving people (Pirkei Avot 1:12).

AGADDIC TRADITION

"**B**rother, why do you cry?" Reb Zusia asked his brother, Reb Elimelech, after they had been unjustly arrested. Reb Elimelech pointed to a pail of waste in the corner of the jail cell. "Jewish law forbids one to pray in a room filled with such repulsive odor," he said. "This will be the first day in my life in which I have not prayed. How can I begin my day without connecting to God?"

"You have already made your connection with God," Reb Zusia said. "It might not be quite where you wanted it, but it is here. If you truly want to make your divine connection, you must be happy with the opportunity God has given you."

With these words, Reb Elimelech's heart filled with joy. The idea that a pail of excrement could create a new type of relationship with God was such a revelation that he began to dance. Soon, both brothers grabbed the pail and danced with it in celebration. Their non-Jewish cellmates joined in.

Hearing the ruckus, guards soon appeared. "What is going on?" they yelled.

"We have no idea!" the prisoners said.

"They're happy because of the pail," sneered the guards. "We'll show them!"

The guards removed the pail from the cell. "All bathroom business will take place down the hall," they said.

Reb Zusia turned to Reb Elimelech and said: "And now, my dear brother, you can begin your prayers."

ACTIVITY 2

1. What are the dangers of feeling contentment regardless of the circumstances? _____
_____

2. Was the brothers' behavior a mere ruse to remove the pail? Would the message of the story be stronger if the guard had not taken the pail away? _____
_____

3. Describe an instance when you transformed an obstacle into an opportunity by changing your attitude. _____
_____

SAMEACH B'CHELKO SUPERSTAR

When **Dr. Rahamim Melamed-Cohen** stumbled over his own feet in 1993, he shrugged it off. "Everyone trips occasionally," he thought.

But soon he felt weakness in his hands and shoulders. He fell down the stairs while at work. Once he fell on his back like a beetle and couldn't get up.

A father of six children and a pioneer in special education programs in Israel, Rahamim was only 57 years old when he received the diagnosis: He had amyotrophic lateral sclerosis (ALS), also known as Lou Gehrig's disease.

The average life expectancy for a person diagnosed with ALS is three to five years, but Rahamim has lived more than 18 years. Although he is completely paralyzed—he can move only his eyes, and he needs tubes to eat and breathe—Rahamim refuses to complain. He has adapted to his limitations with the use of special technology that recognizes the movement of his eyes. Remarkably, he painstakingly completed eight of his 10 books after the onset of ALS. His heroic achievements prompted Rahamim to say that his ailment has given him the best years of his life.

"I think I understand better than most people how to appreciate the important things in life, and to ignore those things that aren't important," Rahamim said. "I feel that I have a task: to give to other people encouragement and strength."

It isn't just sick or disabled people who can benefit from his experience. "I want the opportunity to convey the message of optimism and that life is holy," he says. "Don't despair, be optimistic, and work on *simchah* (joy) in your heart. No matter what you're lacking, think of what's possible to do in your present situation."

Rahamim admits that finding joy in life after falling ill took effort. Medication only controlled his physical pain.

"The problem is the mental suffering: giving meaning to life and having a will to live," he explains. "It's a matter of education, ethics and worldview. I believe that faith helps patients cope during their illness…Despite my deep belief in God from childhood, I had questions and doubts. Why me? Is this a punishment? But thoughts are one thing and actions are another. Today, I thank the Creator that I have lived as I have, that God gave me strength to work."

Rahamim's blog:
http://www.melamed.org.il/aboutEN.html

Time Capsule: *Sameach*

Personal happiness, our sages explain, bears no relationship to how much money we earn. Hillel taught, "The more possessions, the more worry…" (Pirkei Avot 2:8).
Jewish wisdom throughout the ages has criticized senseless extravagance and recognized the importance of living within one's means.

Question #1: Plagued by Wants

May our Teacher instruct us in this:

My family lives modestly, without complaining about all the luxuries we lack, such as linen clothes, fine shoes, and meat every week.

But recently, those around me have flaunted their wealth so much that I feel insignificant in their presence. I don't know if these troubling thoughts have infected my wife and children, but the thought of them living in a state of constant need plagues me daily. Is it appropriate for me to borrow money to buy a few choice goods?

Response to Question #1: Plagued by Wants

If the matter is as your letter of inquiry states, it seems to us as follows:

Our sages, blessed are they, have stated, 'Who is a wise person? One who sees the consequences of actions.'

Therefore, even if God has been kind and given great wealth, a person should not wear expensive embroidered clothing since that will damage one's soul because it brings a person to arrogance and also incites the Evil Inclination. It causes others, who do not have the means, to imitate such behavior. In the end, they will borrow money and not repay their loans.

adapted from the Chofetz Chaim
(1838-1933)

B'*Chelko* in History

Question #2: Show-off Showdown

May our Teacher instruct us in this:

Recently, bar mitzvah celebrations have become extravagant, including expensive musical performances. These elaborate affairs cause a great deal of envy in those who can least afford such celebrations. As a result, they have assumed tremendous debt to pay for these flamboyant occasions.

Response to Question #2: Show-Off Showdown

To all our brethren who fear God: From the time of our inception as a nation, we were distinguished as a people of spirit and nobility, leading modest and wholesome lives. … "Nothing is more beautiful than modesty," our rabbis proclaimed, and a life of modesty was the crowning pride of our people throughout the ages. As of late, the stress on luxurious living is taking an ever-increasing toll on our time and money, and as a result the health and stability of entire families suffer.

excerpted from a public declaration of the Rabbis of Bnei Brak, Israel
(reprinted in The Jewish Observer June 1971)

ACTIVITY 3

Place a magazine or newspaper ad in the center of the page. Circle the advertising strategies that the persuasion industry uses to tempt you to buy the product, even if you don't need it.

Put your ad here

Bandwagon: Everyone is buying it/using it/doing it.

Testimonial: Celebrities claim the product is good.

Image Advertising: The product is linked to attractive/wealthy people, exotic places, or thrilling activities.

Weasel: Words like "usually" or "chances are" imply results.

Omission: No facts to support the product's claims.

Repetition: Repeating a slogan or promise again and again.

Name-calling: Saying negative comments about competition.

Scale: Resizing the product to make it look bigger or smaller.

WHAT I THINK

Jewish wisdom counsels us to find happiness, satisfaction, and contentment with who we are and what we have.

1. Why is feeling grateful an important first step in adopting the value *sameach b'chelko*?

2. What can you do to develop an attitude of gratitude in your life?

3. Role models inspire us to achieve our goals. Make a list of sameach b'chelko role models and learn about their lives.

4. Make a list of three behaviors you will use to resist feeling jealous when you see friends with possessions you can't afford.

5. Lasting happiness comes from meaningful activity, such as study, prayer, and helping others. Write a list of activities that can help you find lasting happiness.

   1.

   2.

   3.

   4.

Anavah

"**When I get** to heaven, they'll ask me, why didn't you learn more Torah? And I'll tell them that I'm slow-witted. Then they'll ask me, why didn't you do more kindness for others? And I'll tell them that I'm physically weak. Then they'll ask me, why didn't you give more tzedakah? And I'll tell them that I didn't have enough money. But then they'll ask me: If you were so stupid, weak and poor, why were you so arrogant? And for that I won't have an answer."

Rabbi Rafael of Barshad
(19th century)

Humility

Rabbi Rafael identifies arrogance as an especially harmful human trait. In fact, he worries that his feelings of superiority might keep him out of heaven. A close examination of this story, however, raises many questions: Are heaven's gates closed to Rabbi Rafael because his sense of self-importance is **undeserved**? Would the gatekeepers have overlooked his excessive pride if it had been built upon legitimate achievements? Don't people who achieve success deserve to feel pride in their accomplishments and confidence in their abilities?

Judaism recognizes the fine line between arrogance and pride. A moderate amount of pride is an important part of personal dignity and self-esteem. Too much pride, on the other hand, breeds conceit and destroys relationships. How do we prevent legitimate pride from rising into arrogance?

Judaism provides a solution, namely, embracing עֲנָוָה (*anavah*, humility) as a lifestyle choice. Contrary to popular opinion, a humble person is not meek or submissive. When we're humble, we have a balanced view of ourselves. We recognize our talents and our shortcomings. Most importantly, we acknowledge that our abilities are a gift from God.

HUMILITY VS. ARROGANCE

- Humble people say, "I can do that."
- Arrogant people say, "I can do that better than anyone else."
- Humble people say, "I am proud I accomplished that."
- Arrogant people say, "I accomplished that, and everyone is impressed."
- Humble people learn from their failures.
- Arrogant people hide their failures, because they feel ashamed of their mistakes.

ACTIVITY 1

Fill in the boxes below to learn more about humility.

 RT @Micah **You have been told what God requires of you, "to act justly, to love mercy, and to walk humbly with God."** #anavah

List as many synonyms as you can

Humility

Definition

List as many antonyms as you can

Learn about these role models: Moses, David, Akiba

Write a haiku about humility (A haiku is a 3-line poem of 17 syllables—5 in the first line, 7 in the second, and 5 in the third).

What I can do to become more humble:

1.

2.

3.

How Does Your Light Shine?

Just how humble are you? Are you humble without being falsely modest?
Take this quiz and find out!

All summer, you've been trying to master your volleyball serve, and you finally ace it. When the coach cheers you on, you think to yourself:

◆ "Wow, our team really worked that play!"

◆ "Man that took a lot of work! I'm glad I kept practicing!"

◆ Run to share the news with your best friend.

After art class, your teacher tells you he loves the sculpture you made and wants to submit it in a contest. You:

◆ Are totally psyched and can't wait to tell your parents!

◆ Say "thanks!" and tell him you've learned a lot in his class.

◆ Run to share the news with your best friend

For your birthday, your best friend gave you a funky new watch. Everyone keeps admiring it, and you:

◆ Tell them who picked it out and mention what great taste he has.

◆ Shrug it off by saying, "Oh, this watch?"

◆ Show everyone how it glows in the dark, because they might not have noticed.

Your little brother calls in to a radio contest giving away two free tickets to a concert. He answers four of the five questions right, but you give him the last one. When the DJ announces that he's the lucky winner, you:

◆ Run and tell your parents what a great team you two make.

◆ Tell him he never would have won if it weren't for you.

◆ Congratulate him, but insist you get one of the two tickets.

Mostly blue
Warm Sunshine
When you accomplish something, you're the first to say "thank you" to someone who helped you along the way. You've got a great team attitude.

Mostly green
Steady Candle Flame
You have a peaceful inner glow—one of self-satisfaction. You love to share your success with others, but don't feel the need for a lot of attention.

Mostly red
Flashing Neon
When you do something well, you enjoy a little praise and attention. Jewish tradition says there is nothing wrong with being motivated by honor, as long as that's not the main goal.

AGADDIC TRADITION

"**What a brilliant scholar** I've become," thought Rabbi Eleazar, proudly recalling how he had bested his master's arguments during their conversation about Jewish law.

"Shalom aleichem," said a shaggy-haired man, wiping his unkempt beard with his dirty hands. Rabbi Eleazar ignored him.

"Peace unto you, master," said the man again.

Irritated that the stranger had interrupted the memory of his triumph, Rabbi Eleazar scowled. "Are all the people in your town as ugly as you?" he asked.

"Why not ask the artisan who made me?" replied the man.

Eleazar instantly realized his sin. "Please forgive my cruel remark," he answered.

"Only the artisan who crafted my body can forgive your insult."

Rabbi Eleazar followed the man into town, pleading for forgiveness. A crowd greeted them.

"Peace unto you, master," they cried.

"Who are you calling master?" asked the stranger.

"Don't you know the man with you is a great man in Israel?"

The stranger explained what had happened, and the townspeople begged him to forgive Rabbi Eleazar.

"I will forgive him," said the man, "but let him be warned never to treat a fellow human as he did me."

Rabbi Eleazar went immediately to the study hall and taught, "One should be soft like a reed, not hard like a cedar." He realized that pride had the power to harden his heart and make his learning a worthless thing.

ACTIVITY 2

1. What was the tipping point that turned Rabbi Eleazar's legitimate pride into arrogance

_____

_____

2. Eleazar's arrogance stemmed from his intellectual achievements. What other successes is arrogance often built upon? _____

_____

3. As Eleazar felt excessive pride welling up inside him, what could he have done to stop it?

_____

_____

ANAVAH SUPERSTAR

The man who discovered the theory of relativity and received the 1921 Nobel Prize in physics was as famous for his humility as he was for his genius.

Albert Einstein was born to a secular Jewish family in the German Empire in 1879. At age 21, he earned a teaching degree but had a hard time finding a job.

In a letter to his wife, Mileva, in 1901, he wrote: "I will look for a position immediately, no matter how humble it is. My scientific goals and my personal vanity will not prevent me from accepting even the most subordinate position."

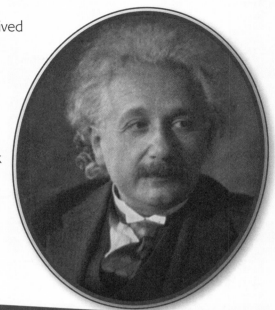

By 1919, Einstein's new theory of relativity shattered the way scientists understood the world. His elegant equation, $E=MC^2$, appeared in newspaper and magazine headlines around the world, catapulting Einstein from near obscurity to instant fame. Although widely acknowledged as the world's smartest person, Albert Einstein remained humble. He refused to allow fame to fundamentally change his simple lifestyle at Princeton University. One historian described him this way:

"Carrying an ice cream cone as he shuffled through town, he would stop to greet children and pet dogs, talk to his barber or other familiar figures he saw in town, and walk about in rumpled clothes and an old leather jacket. Even in his most famous portrait on Time *magazine, Einstein wore an old sweatshirt with a pen attached to the collar with a clip."*

• "A hundred times every day I remind myself that my inner and outer life depends on the labors of other men, living and dead, and that I must exert myself in order to give in the measure as I have received and am still receiving."

• "For the most part I do the thing which my own nature drives me to do. It is embarrassing to earn so much respect and love for it."

• "The highest principles for our aspirations and judgments are given to us westerners in the Jewish-Christian religious tradition. It is a very high goal: free and responsible development of the individual, so that he may place his powers freely and gladly in the service of all mankind."

Time Capsule: *Anavah*

Since biblical days, Judaism's greatest teachers have warned against arrogant behavior. For example, the prophet Jeremiah taught, "Let not wise people glorify themselves with their wisdom. Let not strong people glorify themselves with their strength. Let not rich people glorify themselves with their wealth." (Jeremiah 9:2)

Humility, our tradition says, is the antidote to arrogance.

Question #1: Everyone Is the Same before God

May our Teacher instruct us in this:

My child prepares to leave our home to seek his fortune in the capital city. There, he will be tempted by new ways of life. How can I provide him with the proper advice so he can continue on his righteous path and remember where he came from?

humility

Response to Question #1: Everyone Is the Same before God
If the matter is as your letter of inquiry states, it seems to us as follows:

Counsel your child in a manner similar to these words by our teacher Nachmanides: "Get into the habit of always speaking calmly to everyone. This will prevent you from anger, a serious character flaw which causes people to sin. Once you have distanced yourself from anger, the quality of humility will enter your heart...Why should one feel proud? Is it because of wealth? God makes one poor or rich. (I Samuel 2:7) Is it because of honor? It belongs to God, as we read, Wealth and honor come from You.' (I Chronicles 29:12) So how could one adorn himself with God's honor?

Question #2:
Look Both Ways
May our Teacher instruct us in this:

I worry that my husband is so driven to succeed in his career that he, like many other ambitious people in modern society, spends too much time promoting himself. The slogan of the day is "If you've got it, flaunt it." What can I tell him to keep him from getting too self-involved?

Response to Question #2:
Look Both Ways
If the matter is as your letter of inquiry states, it seems to us as follows:

Remind your husband of Rabbi Simcha Bunim's wisdom, taught to his community in Poland 200 ago: "Everyone must have two pockets, with a note in each pocket, so that he or she can reach into the one or the other, depending on the need. When feeling lowly and depressed, discouraged or disconsolate, one should reach into the right pocket, and, there, find the words: For my sake was the world created.'

But when feeling high and mighty, one should reach into the left pocket, and find the words: 'I am but dust and ashes.'"

ACTIVITY 3

Anavah
Instruction
Manual

*Create your own humility instruction manual. From the list
below, choose the seven behaviors most important to you. See
if your choices match the behaviors recommended by Bachya
ibn Pakuda, the 11th-century Jewish ethical literature pioneer.*

1 Listen to the opinions and judgment of others. _____

2. Don't compliment or flatter another person without meaning it. _____

3. In the face of the universe's infinite beauty, remember your humble origins. _____

4. Acknowledge your mistakes and apologize for them. _____

5. If you have an opportunity to take advantage of another person—don't take it. _____

6. Recognize your shortcomings and do something about them. _____

7. Don't brag or show off. _____

8. Recognize that life is fleeting. _____

9. Act assertive, but not aggressive. _____

10. If a person insults you, don't respond with an insult. Bow out gracefully. _____

11. Never say anything flattering about yourself unless it is necessary (like in a job interview).
    _____

12. Be grateful for all the good in your life. _____

13. Be curious and interested in other people. Ask questions. _____

14. Acknowledge that there is always more to learn. _____

15. Recognize that you can't control unexpected events. _____

16. Accept criticism. Don't get defensive. _____

17. Honor God as the bestower of all the good in your life. _____

WHAT I THINK

Jewish tradition teaches us to recognize that our abilities and special gifts come from God. This acknowledgement enables us to feel pride in our achievements without feeling superior to others.

1. Describe what the world would be like if all people lived by the value of humility. How might society, your school, or even your family function differently?

2. Think of a time when excessive pride caused you to overestimate your ability, and a time when lack of confidence caused you to *underestimate* your ability. What happened? How would you approach that situation now? How could you stem excessive pride or boost your self-confidence?

3. Make a list of people who belong in the Humility Hall of Fame. What can you learn from each person?

4. Create a collage of ways you currently demonstrate humility using images from magazines and newspapers or your own photos. Add three more images that depict ways you would like to demonstrate humility. Use this as your vision board to help humility become part of your everyday life.

CONCLUSION

In *Be Your Best Self*, we learned about four specific Jewish values that provide the foundation for personal growth:

K'vod Habriyot—Individual Dignity
T'shuvah—Returning to Your Best Self
Sameach B'Chelko—Personal Satisfaction
Anavah—Humility

You've been inspired by men and women who exemplify these values, and you've learned from Jewish history and our Aggadic tradition. You've had the opportunity to see how well you apply these values in your life today, and you've given careful consideration to how to further improve — how to become your best self.

For each of the values in the chart below, make a list of at least one activity you will undertake to be your best self by applying Jewish values to your everyday life:

Value	To become my best self, I will …	I'll start on this date …	With this activity, I hope to achieve …
K'vod Habriyot			
T'shuvah			
Sameach B'Chelko			
Anavah			

Discuss your action plan with your classmates … and be your best self!